THE FIRST BOOK OF

Greek Myths

RETOLD BY CAROLINE STEEDEN·
ILLUSTRATED BY ROBIN LAWRIE

‖ ·PARRAGON· ‖

This Book
Belongs to

_____

_____

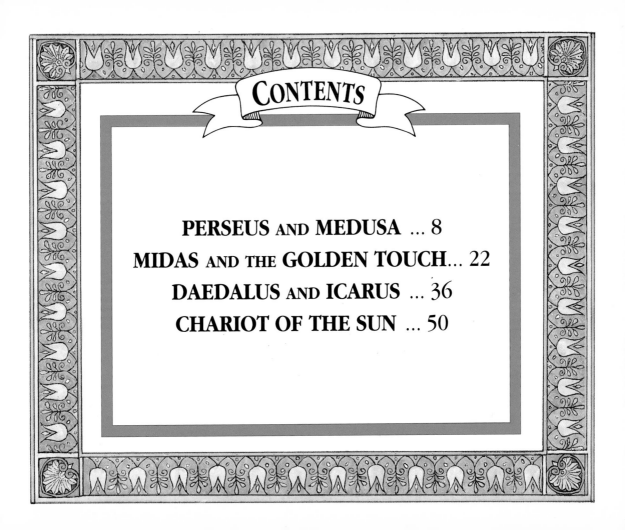

CONTENTS

PERSEUS AND MEDUSA

 stern and hard hearted king, named Acrisius, ruled in the valley of Argos. He had offended the gods, and so one day it had been foretold that he would be killed by his own grandson.

The king had only one child, a beautiful daughter named Danae. In order to stop her marrying and having a son who would one day kill him, King Acrisius locked Danae in a bronze tower, allowing no one at all to visit her. But rumours of her beauty spread, and one night Zeus, father of the gods, came to visit her, disguised as a shower of gold.

In time Danae gave birth to a son, whom
she called Perseus. King Acrisius was
furious and decided he must get
rid of the child.

However, he did not want to make
the gods even angrier by murdering
the baby, so he took his daughter
and the baby down to the
seashore, and sent them
out to sea in a wooden boat.

A PARRAGON BOOK

Published by Parragon Books, Unit 13-17 Avonbridge Trading Estate,
Atlantic Road, Avonmouth, Bristol BS11 9QD
Produced by The Templar Company plc, Pippbrook Mill,
London Road, Dorking, Surrey RH4 1JE

Designed by Janie Louise Hunt
Edited by Caroline Steeden
Printed and bound in Italy
ISBN 1-85813-668-7

Danae was sure she and her child would soon die, and prayed to the gods to help her. As Danae was good and kind, and as Perseus was the son of a god, they were spared. The little boat washed ashore on the island of Seriphos and a kind fisherman called Dictys took them in and looked after them.

It so happened that Dictys was the brother of the King of Seriphos, but the king was not kind and gentle like Dictys. He was a cruel and cunning man named Polydectes. He had taken a liking to Danae and he wanted to marry her, but she did not wish to be his wife. Perseus protected his mother from Polydectes, and took her to live as a priestess at the temple of Athene, to keep her away from the king.

Polydectes was jealous of Perseus, as Perseus was well-loved by the court and the people of the land. He was worried that the people might rise against him, and that

Perseus would take his kingdom, and he was sure that with her son out of the way he had a better chance of persuading Danae to marry him. So Polydectes devised a plan to get rid of Perseus. He told Perseus that people were saying he spent too much time with his mother and other women, and that he was not manly enough. To prove to the people that this was not true he should accept a challenge to demonstrate his courage. The task the king set him was to kill Medusa the Gorgon and bring back her head. Determined to prove his courage and bravery, Perseus accepted the challenge.

Medusa was one of the most terrible and deadly monsters the world had ever known. She had long, curved claws, sharp fangs like a wolf, glaring eyes, and instead of hair, a mass of hissing, writhing snakes. Anyone who looked at her terrible face was instantly turned to stone.

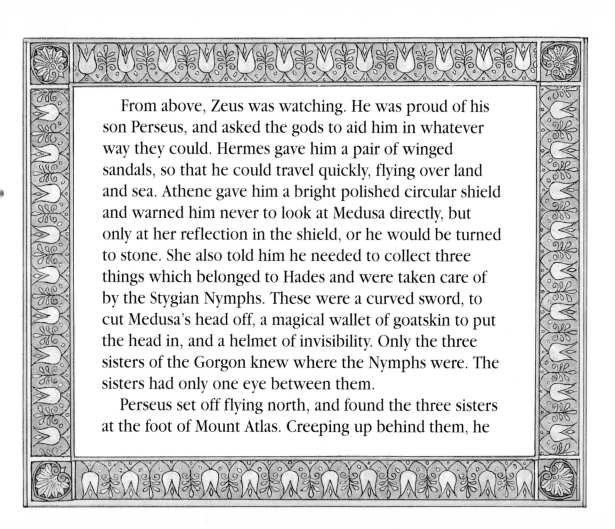

From above, Zeus was watching. He was proud of his son Perseus, and asked the gods to aid him in whatever way they could. Hermes gave him a pair of winged sandals, so that he could travel quickly, flying over land and sea. Athene gave him a bright polished circular shield and warned him never to look at Medusa directly, but only at her reflection in the shield, or he would be turned to stone. She also told him he needed to collect three things which belonged to Hades and were taken care of by the Stygian Nymphs. These were a curved sword, to cut Medusa's head off, a magical wallet of goatskin to put the head in, and a helmet of invisibility. Only the three sisters of the Gorgon knew where the Nymphs were. The sisters had only one eye between them.

Perseus set off flying north, and found the three sisters at the foot of Mount Atlas. Creeping up behind them, he

stole their eye, and wouldn't give it back until they told him where the Nymphs were. He then collected the three things from the Nymphs, and on their instructions flew west to the land of the Hyperboreans, where the Gorgons lived.

He found the Gorgons asleep, amongst the weather-beaten shapes of men and animals turned into stone. Perseus approached carefully, watching Medusa's reflection in his shield. As he drew near, Medusa awoke, and reared up in anger, gnashing her teeth and flashing her eyes. But Perseus' hand was guided by Athene, and with one swift blow he cut Medusa's head clean off! There was a terrible cry that seemed to shake the foundations of the earth. Perseus quickly put the head into the magical wallet, taking care not to look at the head as it could still turn him to stone. Then a miraculous thing happened. From the drops of blood falling from Medusa's body arose the winged horse Pegasus.

The beautiful
white horse
stretched its wings
and flew up into the air
and away into the distance.

The sound of the horse woke the other sleeping
Gorgons, who sprang up and tried to catch Perseus, but
because of his helmet of invisibility, they could not find
him, and he fled to begin his journey home.

His journey was an eventful one, and he still had to face many dangers. He had seen a beautiful princess chained to a rock by the sea, with waves crashing around her. She had been left there as an offering to a sea monster to appease Poseidon, god of the sea, whom her parents had offended. They had claimed their daughter was more beautiful than the Nereids, nymphs of the sea, and so Poseidon had flooded their kingdom. Perseus offered to kill the monster and save their daughter in return for her hand in marriage. He did this by taking to the air and diving on the monster from above, cutting off its head with his sickle. He then freed the princess, Andromeda, married her and took her with him back to Seriphos.

When they arrived Polydectes, the evil king, was about to force Perseus' mother, Danae, into marriage. Bursting into his court room, Perseus confronted the king.

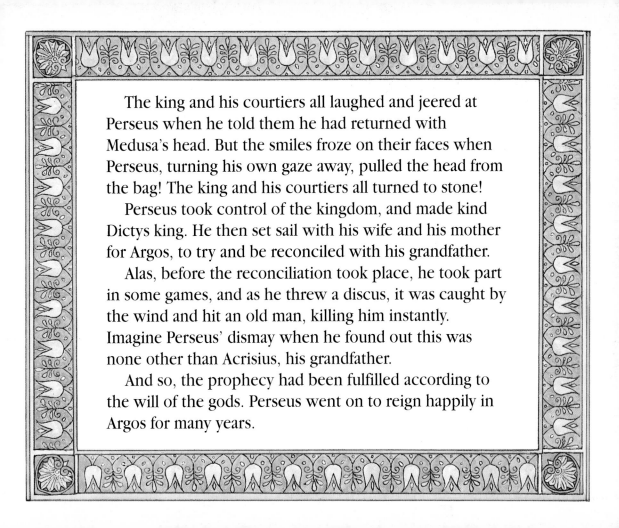

The king and his courtiers all laughed and jeered at Perseus when he told them he had returned with Medusa's head. But the smiles froze on their faces when Perseus, turning his own gaze away, pulled the head from the bag! The king and his courtiers all turned to stone!

Perseus took control of the kingdom, and made kind Dictys king. He then set sail with his wife and his mother for Argos, to try and be reconciled with his grandfather.

Alas, before the reconciliation took place, he took part in some games, and as he threw a discus, it was caught by the wind and hit an old man, killing him instantly. Imagine Perseus' dismay when he found out this was none other than Acrisius, his grandfather.

And so, the prophecy had been fulfilled according to the will of the gods. Perseus went on to reign happily in Argos for many years.

MIDAS AND THE GOLDEN TOUCH

Midas, King of Phrygia, was a foolish and greedy man. He wanted to be the richest man in the world. Some said his love of riches began when he was just a small baby. His nurse had seen a parade of ants crawling up the side of his cradle, each carrying a grain of wheat, which they placed, one by one, into the baby's open mouth. The palace magicians were sent for, and they explained this extraordinary event as a sign of things to come. The grains of wheat stood for riches, so little Prince Midas was sure to become one of the richest kings in the world.

Midas grew into a pleasure-loving king. He filled his palace with beautiful things, and surrounded it with wonderful rose gardens, which he loved to walk in every day.

One morning, as he was walking in his garden, he heard the sound of snoring coming from behind a hedge. He looked over the hedge, and there, fast asleep, was Silenius, who was a great friend and companion to the god Dionysus. Dionysus and his friends were well-known for their rowdy behaviour. Silenius was sleeping off the effects of too much wine. He had stumbled into Midas's rose garden after leaving the feasting the night before.

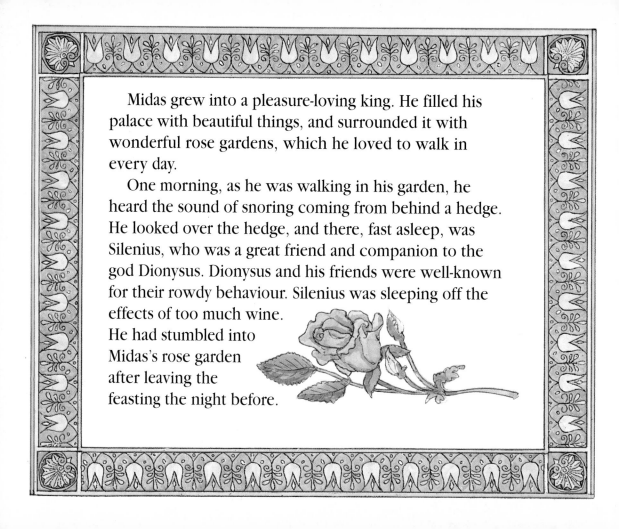

Midas chuckled, as he could
see Silenius enjoyed a life of
pleasure just like him. The king invited Silenius to stay at
his palace, and for a whole week they feasted late into the
night, and Silenius entertained the king with lively stories.

Meanwhile, the god Dionysus had become worried
about his friend, and sent out servants to find him. They
were pleased to find him safe, in good health, and
enjoying the king's hospitality.

Silenius thanked the king for his kindness and returned with the servants to Dionysus. The god was delighted at the safe return of his friend, and sent messengers to King Midas offering him a reward for looking after Silenius so well.

"Ask for anything you wish, your Highness," they told him, "and your wish will be granted."

Now Midas, being a greedy and foolish man, did not stop to think before making his wish. Although he was already rich enough to have anything he wanted, he wanted to be even richer!

"Give thanks to your master Dionysus," he told the messengers, "and tell him that my dearest wish is that everything I touch should turn to gold."

Dionysus knew that King Midas would soon regret his wish, but he decided to teach him a lesson, and granted his wish at once.

Midas could hardly wait to try out his new gift. He reached out and touched a vase of flowers — instantly it turned to gold! Then he touched a chair, which became a solid golden throne. He touched a table, a column, a wall-hanging. Laughing, he ran through the palace, from room to room, touching everything he saw and watching in amazement as everything he touched turned to gold!

Midas ordered that a sumptuous banquet be prepared for that evening, to celebrate his good fortune and give thanks to Dionysus, god of feasting and merriment.

"Here's to Dionysus," he toasted, lifting a wine goblet — but as soon as the wine touched his lips, it turned to a stream of liquid gold! Midas was horrified! He picked up an apple — that too turned to gold, and so did bread, meat — in fact everything he touched! Angrily he pushed away the servant, who stood waiting at his side. At once, a golden statue appeared where once the living man had been!

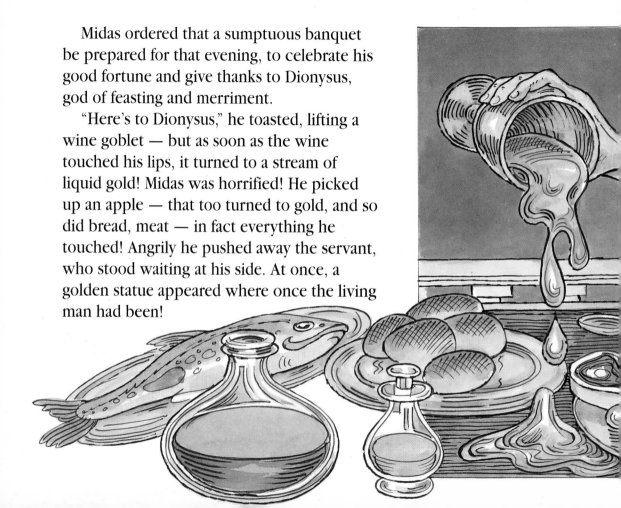

Midas was very upset. He realised he would soon die of hunger and thirst, unless he did something fast! He held his head in his hands and cried, "What a fool I was to ask for such a gift! What good is all this gold to me if I die of thirst and hunger?"

So Midas raised his arms to the sky and tearfully begged Dionysus to take away the power he had granted. Dionysus was a kind god, and he agreed to release Midas from his wish. "He has learned his lesson," thought Dionysus. "Perhaps he will not value gold so highly from now on."

Dionysus told Midas to go to the river Pactolus and bathe in its waters. Midas hurried to do as he was told, and after bathing in the river, found to his relief he no longer had the golden touch, and he had also lost all desire for riches. The sands of the river bed gleamed with gold from that time onwards and King Midas vowed to behave very differently in future.

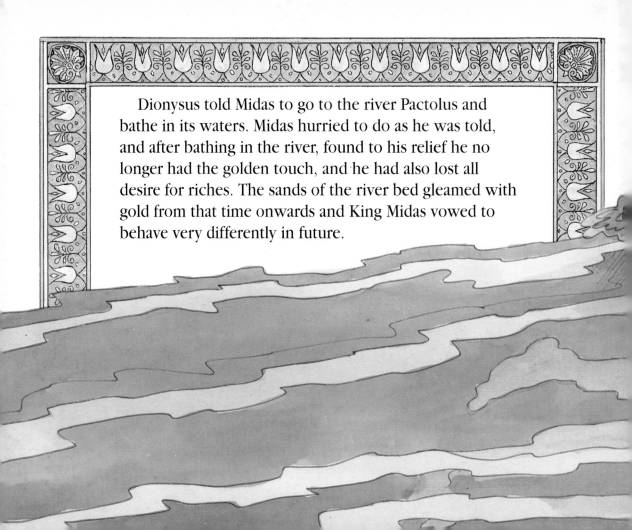

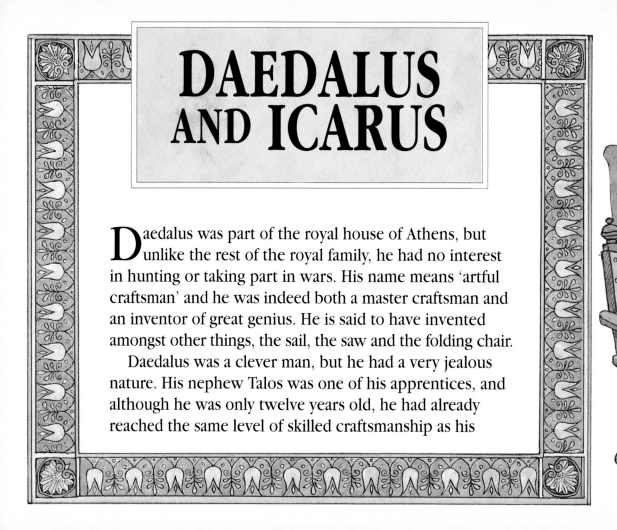

DAEDALUS
AND ICARUS

Daedalus was part of the royal house of Athens, but unlike the rest of the royal family, he had no interest in hunting or taking part in wars. His name means 'artful craftsman' and he was indeed both a master craftsman and an inventor of great genius. He is said to have invented amongst other things, the sail, the saw and the folding chair.

Daedalus was a clever man, but he had a very jealous nature. His nephew Talos was one of his apprentices, and although he was only twelve years old, he had already reached the same level of skilled craftsmanship as his

uncle, and was developing a growing reputation in Athens. Daedalus became unbearably jealous, and taking Talos up to the roof of Athene's temple on the Acropolis, toppled him over the edge. His crime was soon discovered however, and Daedalus, and his son Icarus, were banished to Crete, where King Minos was delighted to welcome so skilled a craftsman.

Daedalus designed many marvellous buildings for King Minos, the most famous of which was called the Labyrinth. This was a building with hundreds of winding halls and a maze of passages so complicated that no one who went in there could ever find their way out again. The Labyrinth was built to house the Minotaur. This terrible creature had the head and shoulders of a bull, and the body of a man, and it fed upon human flesh.

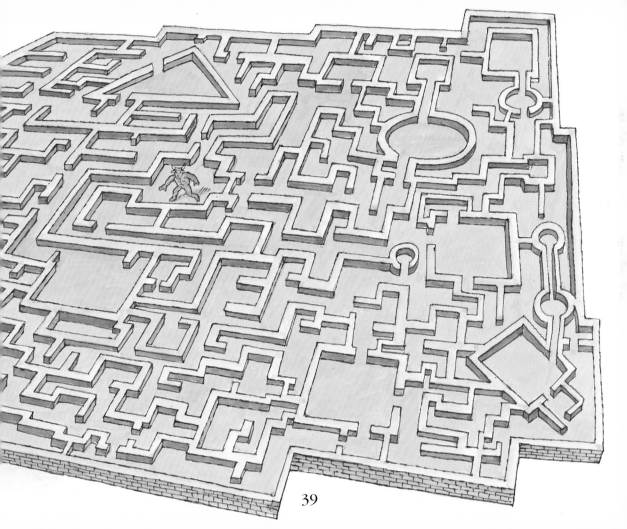

King Minos's son had been killed in Athens in a jealous plot, as he had beaten the Atheneans at the athletic games held there. King Minos had swiftly taken revenge for his son's murder, leading his army in a merciless attack and crushing the city relentlessly, until the city elders agreed to send seven youths and seven maidens as a yearly sacrifice. These poor victims were then let loose in the Labyrinth where they were eaten by the Minotaur.

One year, Daedalus cousin Theseus was amongst those chosen to be sacrificed to the Minotaur. Daedalus helped his cousin to escape by giving him a ball of fine but indestructible thread, which he unravelled as he made his way into the Labyrinth. He killed the Minotaur with a charmed sword, then followed the thread back to the entrance.

King Minos was furious when he discovered Daedalus betrayal, and he imprisoned Daedalus and his son Icarus in the Labyrinth. He worried they might escape from there, however, and so he put all ships under military guard, so they could not leave Crete, and offered a reward for their capture, should they escape.

But Daedalus was determined to escape, and being a brilliant and inventive man, he soon thought of a way to do so. He spent hours studying birds, and the way in which they used their wings in flight. Then out of a pile of feathers he made two sets of wings, welding them together with thread and melted wax. He did this with such skill that the wings looked exactly like those of a giant bird. Deciding it was time to make their escape from Crete, he fastened the wings to his and Icarus's arms. Turning to his son with tears in his eyes he said,

"Icarus, my son, listen carefully to my words. Once we are airborne you must follow closely behind me until we reach the shores of Athens. Do not fly too high, or the sun will scorch your feathers, or melt the wax of your wings. Do not fly too low, or the sea mist will dampen your wings and make them too heavy for you to lift."

With that, Daedalus rose into the air, with Icarus following closely behind.

As they flew away from the island of Crete, the fishermen, shepherds and ploughmen who gazed up and saw them mistook them for gods. Even the king's guards were too amazed by the sight to fix arrows in their bows. Icarus was thrilled to be flying like a bird, swooping and soaring high above the Aegean Sea.

They flew past the islands of Naxos, Delos and Paros, and were making good progress, when Icarus, carried away by his new-found power, disobeyed his father's instructions and began soaring towards the sun.

Higher and higher he flew, until the sun's hot rays began to melt the wax and then down Icarus tumbled, plunging to his death in the deep waters that have since become known as the Icarian Sea. When his father turned to look for him, he saw nothing but scattered feathers floating on the sea below. Daedalus recovered his son's body and took it to an island nearby, where he buried it before continuing on his journey. The island is now known as Icaria.

Daedalus flew on to Sicily where he was warmly welcomed by King Cocalus, and he remained there designing and erecting many fine buildings. When this news reached Crete, King Minos was furious, and he set out at once to demand Daedalus' surrender. However, Cocalus's daughters did not want to lose Daedalus, who made them many beautiful toys, and so together they concocted a plan.

While Minos was taking a bath, they poured hot pitch on him through a pipe they had fixed in the roof, and he suffered a terrible death.

His body was returned to the Cretans, with the story that he had tripped and fallen into a cauldron full of boiling water. He was buried with great pomp and ceremony. Daedalus remained living happily and peacefully in Sicily.

CHARIOT
OF THE SUN

Phaethon was the son of Clymene the Sea Nymph, who was one of the fifty daughters of Nereus the Sea God. His father was Helios, the god who drove the Chariot of the Sun from east to west across the sky each day, bringing light and warmth to the world. Every evening Helios would return to his home in the east, driving his chariot and team onto a golden ferry boat, and sailing home along the Ocean stream, which flows around the world.

His chariot was made of solid gold and was drawn by four beautiful wild horses, with flowing golden manes.

Helios wore a golden helmet, decorated with dazzling jewels which reflected such brilliant rays of light that people had to shade their eyes from them.

Phaethon was brought up in Egypt by his mother, and grew into a handsome boy. He was very proud to have an immortal god as his father, and loved to boast of his divine birth. However, his friends did not believe that Helios was his father, and teased Phaethon, saying he was just trying to make up an excuse for not having a father. This made Phaethon very angry, and he decided that he must do something to prove to them that he was telling the truth. He would visit his father and ask him a favour which would leave no doubts in their minds.

He went to his mother and told her of his decision, and she replied that he must travel far, to the land in the east where the sun rises, and take with him a pearl from the ocean's floor, which Helios had given to her. He had put one of the sun's rays into it to make it shine like no other pearl on earth, and by this sign he would recognise his son.

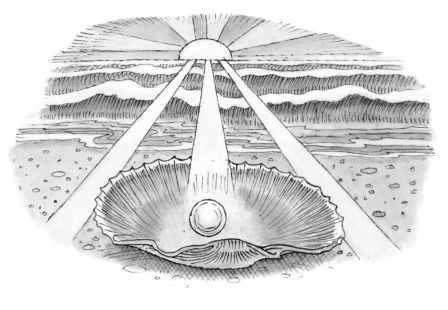

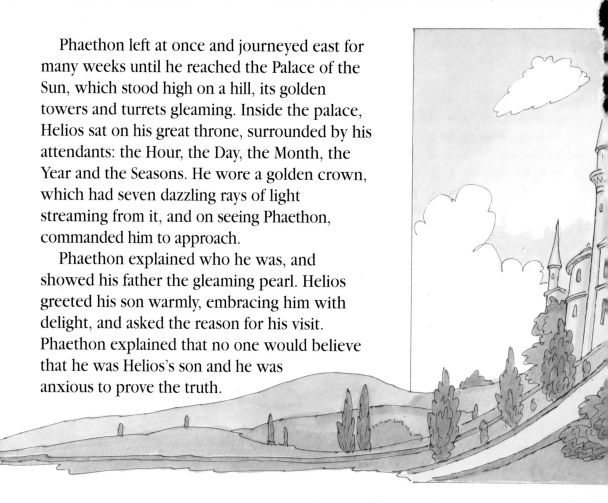

Phaethon left at once and journeyed east for
many weeks until he reached the Palace of the
Sun, which stood high on a hill, its golden
towers and turrets gleaming. Inside the palace,
Helios sat on his great throne, surrounded by his
attendants: the Hour, the Day, the Month, the
Year and the Seasons. He wore a golden crown,
which had seven dazzling rays of light
streaming from it, and on seeing Phaethon,
commanded him to approach.

Phaethon explained who he was, and
showed his father the gleaming pearl. Helios
greeted his son warmly, embracing him with
delight, and asked the reason for his visit.
Phaethon explained that no one would believe
that he was Helios's son and he was
anxious to prove the truth.

His father gave his word at once to do anything he could to help, but he was ill-prepared for the request his son then made: "Father, let me take your place for just one day and drive your chariot across the heavens, so that all my friends may see me and know that I truly am your son."

Helios held his head in his hands groaning in distress. "What you ask is impossible. Even the gods would not ask such a thing, for they know the skill, experience and great strength that such a task calls for. I have made a rash promise, and you have made a dangerous wish that I cannot grant." Phaethon begged and pleaded with his father, who was firm, telling him of all the dangers and difficulties of the journey. "My horses are wild and untamed. Even I can scarcely control them. You must release me from my promise." But Phaethon was determined and eventually his father agreed reluctantly to honour his promise.

Dawn was fast approaching when Phaethon climbed into the sun god's chariot. Helios placed his golden crown of fire on his son's head, and gave him a few last words of advice. "Take great care, my son. Hold the reins firmly, and keep to the broad path. The horses know their way and will travel fast without encouragement. If you go too high you will burn the homes of the gods, and if you go too low you will scorch the earth."

Phaethon cracked his whip and the horses leapt into the night. As they climbed steeply upwards towards the heavens, the first rays of their light touched the hills in the east, then spread to the valleys below. They had not gone far, when the horses sensed that the strength and determination of Helios was not there to guide them, and, tossing their golden manes, they broke away from the well-worn path, and plunged wildly towards the earth.

Phaethon had no strength to control them, and he looked in terror as the earth came rushing towards him, with the fiery chariot swerving from side to side beneath him. How he wished he had listened to his father and not been so proud and stubborn.

As the Chariot of the Sun swooped low over the earth trees withered in the scorching heat, fields of corn smouldered, and towns and cities were set ablaze. Mountains burned and the fertile land of Egypt became a desert.

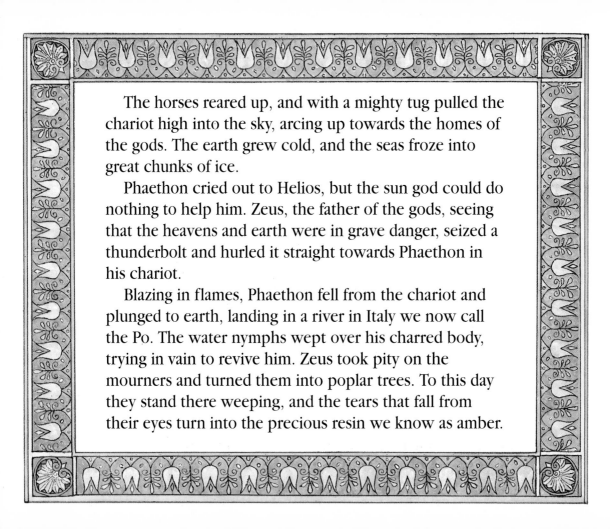

The horses reared up, and with a mighty tug pulled the chariot high into the sky, arcing up towards the homes of the gods. The earth grew cold, and the seas froze into great chunks of ice.

Phaethon cried out to Helios, but the sun god could do nothing to help him. Zeus, the father of the gods, seeing that the heavens and earth were in grave danger, seized a thunderbolt and hurled it straight towards Phaethon in his chariot.

Blazing in flames, Phaethon fell from the chariot and plunged to earth, landing in a river in Italy we now call the Po. The water nymphs wept over his charred body, trying in vain to revive him. Zeus took pity on the mourners and turned them into poplar trees. To this day they stand there weeping, and the tears that fall from their eyes turn into the precious resin we know as amber.